Borrowed Dress

THE FELIX POLLAK PRIZE IN POETRY

The University of Wisconsin Press Poetry Series

Ronald Wallace, General Editor

Now We're Getting Somewhere • David Clewell
Henry Taylor, Judge, 1994

The Legend of Light • Bob Hicok
Carolyn Kizer, Judge, 1995

Fragments in Us: Recent and Earlier Poems • Dennis Trudell
Philip Levine, Judge, 1996

Don't Explain • Betsy Sholl
Rita Dove, Judge, 1997

Mrs. Dumpty • Chana Bloch
Donald Hall, Judge, 1998

Liver • Charles Harper Webb
Robert Bly, Judge, 1999

Ejo: Poems, Rwanda, 1991–1994 • Derick Burleson
Alicia Ostriker, Judge, 2000

Borrowed Bress • Cathy Colman
Mark Doty, Judge, 2001

Borrowed Dress

Cathy Colman

The University of Wisconsin Press

The University of Wisconsin Press
1930 Monroe Street
Madison, Wisconsin 53711

www.wisc.edu/wisconsinpress/

3 Henrietta Street
London WC2E 8LU, England

5   4   3   2   1

Printed in Canada

Library of Congress Cataloging-in-Publication Data
Colman, Cathy A.
Borrowed dress / Cathy A. Colman
    pp.   cm. —(Felix Pollak prize in poetry)
    ISBN 0–299–17540–5 (cloth: alk. paper)
    ISBN 0–299–17544–8 (pbk.: alk paper)
    I. Title. II. Felix Pollak prize in poetry (Series)
PS3603.056 B6   2001
811.'6—dc21   2001002002

for my mother, Joan, and grandmother, Marcella

to the memory of Donald Berry (1958–1988)

Speaking always implies a treason.

—ALBERT CAMUS

Contents

Acknowledgments

Grateful acknowledgment to the editors of the following publications in which these poems first appeared, sometimes in different versions:

Colorado Review: "Deliverance"
Hyper Age Magazine: "Annunciation," "Sleep," "The Sybil"
Mudfish: "Pyro"
Quarterly West: "Reasons Not to Have You"
Spoon River Poetry Review: "Breaking and Entering"
The Southern Poetry Review: "Newton's Law"
The Valley Contemporary Poets Anthology: "Seeds"
Inking Through the Soul: Writers on Writing from Tarcher/Putnam:
    "Mistress"
"Annunciation," "Sleep," and "The Sybil" won the Ascher Montandon
    Poetry Prize.

I would like to express my deep gratitude to my family for their love and support during the incubation of this book: Henry Colman and Donna Brainard, Richard Colman and Rocky Clair, Donald Hoytt, Bonnie Roche, and Shana and Phil Buckman. So many friends have helped me, too many to mention here, but I'm especially grateful to Madelaine Brody, for her extraordinary skills at both editing and friendship; and to Brett Taylor and Dick Halligan for their generosity and loyalty.

This book would not have been born without the specific help, encouragement and inspiration of writers Elena Karina Byrne, Leslie Campbell, Tracy DeBrincat, Jeffrey McDaniel, Donna Prinzmetal, Judith Serin, Judith Taylor, and David Warfield. Many thanks to Molly Bendall and Carol Muske-Dukes for their insightful comments on the finished manuscript and to Stan Rice for starting it all.

Je vous remercie profondément: Dr. Michael Beckwith, Jackie Dennis, Fred Dewey, and especially Eileen Paris.

My gratitude to Richard Misrach for his incomparable vision and kind permission to reproduce the cover photograph.

I

THIS HAD SOMETHING TO DO WITH RADIANT LINEN

Zygote

I did my best
when I was young, saying the names
of saints in spring's green office.

What will happen is part drowse, part thunderhead,
branches that peel their own skins like penitents.
What will happen when I'm counted, thumbprint

and tongue, upstaged by a tiny contortionist
who came into the world backward and upside-
down, tattooed with luck? Who could count

every flicker and sheath, measure the swarm
that covers the deck with sticky kisses? I tell you,
what will happen is that winter's gaunt prodigies

will disappear. There will be an imitation
of weeping, just to keep me happy, because,
after all, I *am* a slave, and what will happen is

that every hook will find its eye, all over
the continent, and I'll get smacked by the boomerang
of desire and the monsoon will hit and where I place

the oar there will be a spoon whose mouth of glare
says oh, oh and everything I eat voraciously
will be itself voracious.

Sleep

I wake suddenly from a small red sleep
as if the darkness were oil rising up to my eyes.

I'd give almost anything to go back.
Even dream the one about the lost wallet,

the forgotten locker combination, teeth falling out—
even the hanged woman, my double,

with her blue sash noose, her Raggedy Ann dress.
Entombed in my bed,

the sheets like marble in moonlight,
my rebellious heart beats too fast,

an adolescent fist
dipped in red sealing wax.

I can sleep late, I tell myself,
because I have no children.

Only dust and the sly, early-morning furniture.
I have no husband

but the black mountain from whose shoulders
I can see the river shining like tin.

What kind of offering can I make to you, Sleep?
Haven't I already given you more than I have given anyone?

Deliverance

Maybe when the ink dries
and the Bishop of Loneliness leaves town

Maybe when the thunder stops rehearsing
and the latticework of frost lifts

and seeds bump up through the earth
Maybe when the blunt-featured face of Dread

fades from the window
and the bare fields are revealed

as the origins of sight
Maybe when we recover the body we call

god or dog or King of Dogs
and the day is unwired

from giving and receiving
Maybe when the minutes lose their tethers

and the white ammonia of the mind
finally burns itself out

Impermanence in Orange

Remember us, impermanence:
sky imprinted with the scumbled

drawing of the master,
oriental garden lacquered with moonlight

and shadow like midnight on a cruise ship.
Remember us, darkness,

always-invited-to-the-party-
light. Remember us, nothing.

Patient, necessary
in-between. Remember us,

ocean, turn your translucent pages,
burn our throats.

Forgive us, music
which is like time transfigured by water.

Remember us, surprise-in-forest
tiny, orange salamander

becoming the leaf,
thrown into the jackpot of autumn.

Remember us, wrecked bodies
of cars, rusting so prettily you almost

flower, perfume the delusion-
engendering air of August.

Remember us, dream-torn, jammed
into that traffic, trying to leave our bodies.

Remember us, mystery,
our rooms haunted by the argument

of space/time et cetera. Remember us,
turning doorknobs we thought

would get us into heaven, or at least
a recess from the crush and press,

the life we try to rescue
from the living.

Nothing

God made everything out of nothing.
But the nothingness shows through.
                    —Paul Valéry

This had something to do
with the blush and swap
of a fugitive arrangement,

the addition and subtraction
of heat, a white hoax and a cloud
of blue butterflies. This had something

to do with radiant linen and the swift
inoculations of rain; with siestas that let us
practice oblivion. All the intimate beginnings

now forgotten. Though we are changed
by everything, nothing appears
to move. Why can't we be content

with the nothing that glues it all
together? The rooms of summer filled
with their own furniture, named willow,

chain-link, radish, sorrow, dogwood, utopia?

Annunciation

This is something I need to tell you: a man cries onto a small woman's shoulder on the Pont-Neuf, the way coins stand on end and pigeons are struck dumb in strong sunlight. Poodles carried in handbags have the bemused cloudy eyes of heroin addicts; women with faces like blanched almonds; and pigs, always pigs, hanging in the shop windows. And the way fear keeps surprising the body, when lips warily licked by their own tongue grow suddenly unfamiliar.

It is true, nothing is familiar to us. A shape beckons eerily from the bedroom's twilight and is revealed as a jacket askew on its hanger. And you, who were most familiar, have become glasses glinting in night traffic, unread books. We wait for memory to explain the present.

I walk the Pont d'Archevêché between two views, the infernal-colored sunset making the buildings look fractured, elegant, damned, while the silvery net of evening veils the sweet, demented faces of gargoyles, their expressions softened by age.

It's charming really, to live with no past tense, paintings you look at until the moment you cease to exist and a door opens at the end of the muddled garden and music crashes in the bushes like a motorcycle.

Then there comes the morning you wake alone in an unfamiliar room, dawn already breathing at the window in its blue suit, the sound of a key's cough in a lock and the delicate accuracy of a faucet tap tap tapping like a small silver cane.

Translating the Future

The past is in the pantry
wolfing cake,
and from a farther room

a phonograph plays "Johnny Angel"
and "Love Me Do."
The past threw its back out

so it has been mostly prone,
waiting for the future
to bring it an ice pack.

I feel sorry for the past
that has no volition,
no immediate liquor of sensation.

I want to comfort it with flowers,
maybe a nice canopy.
That always makes me feel better.

But the past is beside itself,
betrayed, discarded,
its sex a parrot of desire.

As leaves spin, falling to the ground
like unhooked syllables,
I hear it call weakly through the wall.

I was, it says, I was.

Nostalgia of the Infinite

—after De Chirico

Nothing will be as it was, that sweet limbo
    before birth, before the hangover matter
        gave us as we were squeezed through the trigger

of time, just as I was beginning to forget
    about you a little. Forget the science
        by which something is always missing, fields

quaffed of their luster, pins skittering
    to the floor, a sprig of melancholy
        added to the feast. Even when we glimpse

for a moment, the pattern or the wreckage

of the pattern, most of the past is lost;
    is it the present or the future's thirst
        that is never slaked? I haven't slept

in days, just wandered through rooms
    past appliances in their gleaming trances, frost's
        handwriting on the windows, because nothing

will be as it was. Even after energy
    stops hobnobbing with matter,
        and I learn from the constellations a rapt

absence, the urge to give myself away.

Newton's Law

This train is stopped by
a blank page. The watermark:

invisible eye of God. The truth—
or words arranged to look like it—

disappears like scarves of smoke. It all
blends together. Death and the platform,

immortality and dark tickets. On this primary
morning I can smell the word newspaper

on my fingers. And I climb the waffled steel
steps, steam panting beneath my legs

like a hound. History happens so fast; mist
rises from weed-pierced dirt, from the sweet

dawns and backyard carnage of other lives.
In a house, blue curtains inflate like a mystery

moving inside a body. Brick buildings and
billboards advertising milk are whisked away

as we hurtle into winter's bright coma,
into the hocus-pocus of the normal.

II

LIKE FROST ON THE STUBBLE

Mistress

The usual trouble is in the morning light,
the now-or-never part of the day's voice.

The cure?
I have a mistress who retells my stories

in a dishonest but more entertaining way;
who balances pieces of camouflage on her lips

and calls it cake; who sleeps like a knife;
whose iridescent veins are a map of the Russian steppes.

If I want dreams, I'll ask for them.
Right now I'm trying to get The Ineffable to talk.

Threatening to leave it in a men's room
in Atlantic City. I know I shouldn't

use force. But soon I'll hear my mistress
scuffing down the hall

in her paper shoes.

Acrostic at Dinner

Carried along by excess,
Art is what happens by accident.
The tablecloth whisked from under the dishes.
Harm and restitution in one clear act.
Your guests bark with laughter.

Can yearning get confused with dessert?
Orange ice, the chill, shapely tower of it!
Like a miniature citadel.
Meaning: a tongue, a pressure on
All the right places, to consume
Not what we love but what could possibly love us.

Life Drawing

Art is a lie that makes us see the truth.
—Pablo Picasso

—the smocked instructor fashioned a blue drape behind me, said
he was up all night thinking of poses. He was famous for his art
collection and for the definitive book on Cézanne's composition,
the way he juxtaposed color planes to create depth in a new way, a
book that Ginsberg read in the fifties inspiring him to write
"Howl" in which he put "hydrogen" and "jukebox" together to
form the image "crack of doom on the hydrogen jukebox" but I
wasn't thinking about this as I hung

from ladders, naked, sat idle with a turban on my head at the bath,
with that slightly bored look of inward longing, the cold chalky
floor under my feet. I could almost feel them sketching my breasts,
leaving out my nose, the ubiquitous bowl of fruit echoing the
curved shapes against the rectilinear:

my head had solidity, the instructor told me. Perhaps the smudged
charcoal drawings would tell me something I didn't know: who I
was when the details were still separate. I liked the idea of the non-
hierarchical picture plane in Cézanne, every part equal to every
other part, like a story with no plot, my head equal to my cunt, my
hips to my feet, but in Degas it was the attitude, the moment when
you were fixed in time before the light changed.

—this was all years before I stumbled through the Hopper show in
New York at the Whitney, betrayed by a man, and I wondered
does the psyche produce the objects of alienation in these paintings
or do the objects project their solitariness, the *lost condition*
common to all objects, into the psyche? And I thought that the
people in these

paintings took on the status of objects not because there was no feeling between them but because the objects themselves mirrored *feeling that once was,* the walls, moldings, curtains saturated with loss, with no ability to communicate their distress like the helplessness of a room where a murder has been committed,

and how strange it was that he went off with a woman who looked like a study for my portrait, an orchid that would take ten years to bloom, and how I stared so long at Cézanne's painting of *Rocks at Fontainebleu* that it began to force its violence and restlessness on me until there was no difference between us, just as there is no difference, sometimes, between truth and the imagination that eats what it can't touch,

and then suddenly I came back to myself because the art students had sprayed the drawings with fixative and the instructor had dismantled the curtain, the pitcher, the bowl of golden pears and all the shameless apples—

How To

The secret is to rise early.
Listen to liturgical collisions in the jazz riffs.
See how that square of sunlight foreshadows

a bigger radiance in the day.
Drink strong tea. Get up and sing
a lively song. Or reenact Galileo's discovery

of a heliocentric universe. Sorry, I meant
Copernicus. Then peel hard-boiled
eggs that roll wildly around the plate

reminding you vaguely of dating.
Slice the eggs so you're surprised
by the gold coin yolk and how painterly

they look on the blue Fiestaware
next to the Early Girl tomato. Now
you might begin to suspect that

some duty needs to be discharged—phone calls
made, bills paid, or perhaps a fresh
elucidation of Oliver Wendell Holmes's aphorism

"We will twist the tail of the cosmos 'til it squeaks."
But resist these mandates. Just laugh,
like Republicans at welfare.

Sit down at your desk. Whack the piñata of childhood
until something ugly flies out. If you can't
find a subject, stare out the window.

Wait for an image to announce itself, or the mail-
person, whichever comes first. Or use
a phrase from another writer's poem to get going.

For example: "The secret is to rise early."

Dark Painting

The art of unpacking, one by one,
the tired items, sending them off to charity.
Then I can hunker down in my chair

under the plum tree and dream
of the lucid moment—night's intricate
ironwork of trees against sky

and the sky itself with a bit of conflagration
around the edges, a piece of paper on fire.
See how the present

slips away, a dumb show.
It has no desire to record itself.
But the past is vain. Tells its story

over and over. When I was young,
someone was always on her knees
searching for keys or a lost

token. And from the street came the strange
music of saxophones and curses.
High on speed and chaos I'd

wade through darkness, Pompeii's fresco
swarming with maroons and beaten blues,
before I stepped into the black limousine

of sleep, before I felt the sensation again:
all the cells in the body
like card-houses, collapsing. I couldn't see

the pentimento, the original immaculate gesture.
In the Middle Ages they painted people flat
so as not to offend the three-dimensionality of God.

Carp

You rise and fall at will,
       this loveliness we can't have
              but see in flashes, in the rhythm
of an insight. Your delicate, crenellated
              fins like those ribbed petticoats
we had to wear.

Carp, with your golds more precious
       than money, reds that hold dominion
              over rubies, your solemn clown majesty,
your clothes.
              Can you distract us from simple ruthlessness,
like anything that must flatter to survive?

Carp, I have loved you for your arrogant over-
       dressing, your tangerine and cream
              sequined gowns, the way you suck insistently
on my finger, seeking nourishment where
       there is none. Dear Carp: your hunger,
so much like mine.

When I'm Dead,

I won't mind
the hangman's hands,
the weightlessness my body has

after dropping its thirsty disguise.
I won't whine
or talk about happiness,

that houseguest who smiles
amiably after using all
the hot water.

When I'm dead, I won't see angels
disappear through keyholes.
Won't see their shrouds

like frost on the stubble.
They'll stay around longer, so I can
get a good look at them.

No heads will roll or appear
on pikes at dawn. When I'm dead,
I won't squander the nickel riches

of the lonely, scream "tyrant"
twenty times a day. Dead,
I'll be far away from

my fear as a calendar is
from lived time. Then you'll know me
as you never did before.

And I'll remember how it was
to be alive down here: paper and dust,
everyday deities.

Virtù

... and his [the artist's] virtù, the unique energetic signature
of all he does ... the radiant node from which, and through
which ideas are constantly rushing.
                    —Hugh Kenner paraphrasing Ezra Pound

Not to be known, I fall
    bodiless, back into time, wordless
        into the future's corridor

of unblinking light. Instrument
    from a lost world, I have no true
        mirror: sun effaced behind her mesh

veil. I am known only by The Unknowable,
    who is everywhere and nowhere, invisible
        in this same unholy fix. I don't know

how to unearth the torqued and burnished
    relic, to receive the vision, to know dissonance
        in its rent form, beautiful ruin. After all,

summer is blue at heart. Even the branches trace
    their untranslatable signatures on the pane. Not to be
        called by any other name, though I name

myself: bracken that complicates by the river,
    nothing's euphoria, virtù's lover.

III

WHERE I BALANCED ON THE WEAKEST LIMBS

Against History

Nothing has prepared me for the past:
Vermeer, but with something terribly wrong.
The rain-colored curtains, the shy accountability
of mirrors, her vanity table with its miniature
city of glass—objects eternal before the painter
painted them. Before memory remade my parents'
room with bandages of light. There's no forgetting
the wrecked surfaces of desire, the small violence
within—torn narcissus, bald stump. There's no
forgetting her mirages, his suitcase
shining like polished boots. Before light swallowed
the details and spit them out.

The Sybil

There is death in clocks, in raw chicken, in certain unmentionable vegetables, in aluminum, in rows of similar houses, in a piece of hair coiled in a motel sink. There is death in a sigh, a blown kiss; death in translation, in numbers, in the germs that cover every available surface, death in the filthy Ladies' Rooms of train stations, death in happiness that angers the vengeful gods, death in surrender to water, death in surrender.

My mother predicted my death before I was born. In addition, she predicted the death of reason and the first real tragedy of spring. She counted on the insane wisdom of stars to control our destinies. She predicted death from color television, from black jellybeans, from cats that touched encephalitic birds, from pools of mosquitoes, from microwaves, from cancer left on toilet seats.

My mother predicted my death in many places. She predicted my grave would be a vacant lot surrounded by piles of disgorged rocks, or the thumping, ignominious sea: my skin turned to silt, my hair waving, insensible as seaweed. Or that I would be scattered like Osiris when the airplane cracked open in the sky.

My mother predicted my death in many ways, so that my hands were always tied behind my back, ready for execution. She predicted death from falling, from swimming, from driving with neighbors. She predicted my death by a mad strangler who would use nylon stockings not unlike the ones in her second bureau drawer, soft tentacles around my small neck.

My mother predicted my death because somehow she knew my genes were encoded with desire for the impact, for example, of a concrete wall whose whiteness sang to me at night when I drove, and for the men who said they were my father and took me underground, bathed me with adulterous hands as I lay on my side like a fish.

What if I welcomed my death? Walked out into the suave,
dangerous night with its hunks of obsidian, replicating shadows.
What if I walked outside, half-naked, fumbling for my keys, not
locking the car doors? What if I let a stranger follow me home or
climbed the black tree of passion, branch by branch, to the top,
where I balanced on the weakest limbs, listening for them to break?

What if I woke one morning, suddenly safe on the barge of my
body, and called out to her my betrayal: *This death*, mother, *this
death that has been closer than breathing, closer than hands and
feet, does not exist!*

The Search for Meaning in the Backyard

once solved, would prove its existence:
    the yellow mystery in each flowerlet, the spiky scent of wild
onion grass that secreted summer and its feast of hours
    or the tomato plants that manufactured their own green dust.

Because I was the oldest I had to find the meaning first,
    from the heat and earth-slant, from night's umbrella
with its sharp tip ready to blind me.
    But we could dig to China

together, find it in the gold dirt, the mahogany dirt,
    what was under the willows, their unfurled flags of shadow,
deep wells of ink. We could startle each other
    out of childhood, the way

the metal clothesline smelled like winter with its fleshy
    berries not yet out. The way dusk came to us
with sharp stones and our names
    when called sounded like the cries of water. I still lie
      in this dark and listen to what made us.

—for my brother, Richard

Just Add Water

I grew from hair, twine, excess salt,
my left breast Selfishness

my right breast Will
while my mother spoke strenuously

of the importance of never appearing
in *deshabille*.

I marveled over the miraculous
birth of my sea monkeys, just drop

the tablets in water and the colored,
swimming creatures lived! Surely this

was a sign. A sample kit from
the glorious future which was,

at that very instant,
readying itself to receive me.

Pyro

—for the arsonist

My father videotaped everything.
Not just for insurance purposes.
He videotaped the burning
and the aftermath

so he could watch it later.
He sat on his haunches in the trillium,
staring at the skeleton of his Cadillac.
A gaggle of small boys

sifted through the carrion. Everything
looked like the blunt, stained end
of a weapon. Somewhere in the layers
was the rosewood box that contained

the ashes of his greyhound, Peaches,
fried twice; his collection of celebrity
dentures; the photographs of the B-17
bombers. I didn't see my brother at his house—

I watched the video of my brother's visit.
My father pans the camera up, up.
And on the video I see
that the blue sky chips away like personality,

and behind it the universe is black,
like the back of a mirror.

Breaking and Entering

I am tired of ordering things. The coquettish spoons, the sly knives
on the right, the sentry forks guarding against insurrection, the
glass full of holy water that has been purified of desire. It's the
smallest possible point I live on like a cannibal. I eat that which is
like me, drink the salty blood from the platter. The day swallows
its materials—time—whole while I wait to give birth to something
stainless, something that will float, instead of this longing that
dresses up like lust, that clamors for supper, that always wants the
best table, the most expensive item on the menu. The waiter brings
me the bill like an affidavit. He reads me my rights. I have nothing
to say. This is how I know I can begin telling the truth.

* * *

In the beige living room next to the mahogany piano, I
accidentally stabbed my father with a scissors while trying to shirr
a ribbon. I couldn't escape through the attic with the ball gowns in
trunks, through the crawl space where the baby rabbit died.
Finally I fled into woods of maple and sycamore, built rooms
under leaves, a new house with better light and air. I had homunculi,
little people I played with, a man and a woman. I made them have
sex, the man on top. They looked like the plaster dolls on my
parents' wedding cake. The bride had a piece of netting glued to
her chestnut pageboy hair. The groom wore a flaking tuxedo and
had surprised, bullethole eyes. But my man and woman had real
skin and they breathed.

* * *

If he had had his way, he would have turned me to salt. Not even
salt itself, but a painting of salt. How soon, by my own hand,
would I have had those two intimate dates below my name, in the
delicate parenthesis that is a life? In secrecy I divine the true

meanings. Bear down on words until blood runs. Is that how to do it? Write with a knife?

* * *

I can see the shapes of the newly dead and the long dead coming to tea. They are, after all, harmless creatures; badly loved for the most part, their graves untended, their mourners self-occupied. They speak to me, not in words, but in the clouds that drift soundlessly, in the wishbones of water that scar the dry dust. When the wound blossoms inside me, when the lawn is eaten by shadows and trees are routinely slaughtered, I step into another room where everything is possible. They prove it to me, the quiet ones who ask for only a little blood to give them strength to sing. I hold the china cup to their lips and the fallen trees rise up and form a language of the future. And my own fortune? Quick, green, and ruthless.

Chinese Takeout

> But the most constant source of enchantment came from the harlequin
> pattern of colored panes . . . the small square of normal, savorless glass
> [was] of all the windows, the pane through which in later years parched
> nostalgia longed to peer.
>
> —Vladmir Nabokov, *Speak Memory*

Warned by the fortune cookie that "Happiness is no laughing matter,"
I saw my childhood through Nabokov's window, longing
with its grape-colored hours, burst thunderstorm, shout
of a commuter train, already into the next

world. What can destiny do but wait, sealed in its sentences, terrible
euphony? It took all my courage to enter
grief and its true object. There's nothing wrong with this. Fathers

and their daughters, daughters
and their lovers, daughters alone.

I'm not afraid of sequence, just consequence.

Paradoxical Undressing

A condition in which some victims of hypothermia who are near death, rip off their clothes when a dilation of constricted blood vessels close to the body's surface produces a sudden sense of heat.

—*Vanity Fair*

Let us assume, for the sake of argument, that you and I
are happy with "the way things are" as we stand
at the lintel of the century, the streets lit
by anarchy and flames. I dream David St. John
tells me, "If you just take Mick Jagger out
of the poem it will be luminous." Like the field
you long for. Like the cows. No, the cows
are another matter. Bloated and ponderous

as a bad allegory. I want to love them but I have to drink
bourbon and smoke Marlboros first because all those
cows are dead, the ones from your childhood farm
I learned about the night we ate steak and you explained
the process of milking. And what good is my love now
to either them *or* you. They say in the city nothing's
easy. When I drive I hear a voice chanting
"here is the tundra, here is the ax" and suddenly I see

that the coral trees on San Vicente have the origin of grief
in their bones, cut so mercilessly they look like they're planted
upside-down. I just want to stop talking about my love
life, which is a cross between rapture of the deep and smoke
inhalation. You're supposed to escape the latter by crawling
belly down along the floor until you can get to an exit.
Aren't things supposed to be rising? Even while
the universe expands and *The New York Times* says that

there are seven known dimensions; that space and time no longer exist. But not to worry, this won't change your daily life one whit. Let us come in from the burning cold, which makes us undress when we are actually freezing, like those who die of hypothermia. Arms outstretched, naked in the snow, their expressions euphoric as if in the throes of sexual ecstasy.

IV

INSIDE, I LED A DOUBLE LIFE

To Heidelberg

Of course we wanted this: how we drifted
from the platform in the avalanche of musk

and overcoats, dissolving into the train, the pantomime
of travelers, the haze of the unforgiven going somewhere

blind. One of us the mute, cheated partner, no one
to instruct us on the protocol. Feverish to alight

on the precise confession that would bring us
closer. Because it was a pilgrimage past the graying

cities rained on by milk and ash, the tombstones
decorated for Christmas, the ravine where a fugitive

knelt all night in dirty water. Of course we wanted this
hurricane of kisses under the bridge, sky filled with gaudy

plumage, all landscape a hallucination, silver traceries
across fields, dark enigma of gathered pines. Sometimes

the landscape seemed to stagger under the burden
of its beauty. Instead of time, *we* were the fluid, obliterating

fix of speed and distance, the fog muzzling other voices,
quieter but unrelenting. What is this tenderness

that invents itself inside a moving train, between
destinations? And lives only upon the sweet blade of ignition,

where we are orphaned from the known,
the dizzying surveillance lights of home.

Seeds

He wants to pick oranges at night.
He unscrews them like light bulbs
from the branches.

When his basket is full he comes in,
his hands sticky with their blood.
They are my neighbor's oranges.

I have pressed my ear
to the earth, heard their fragile
music. Bright seeds.

What is love if I can't
taste it? It makes sex exciting
to lie with a thief.

As if I am the thief.
As if they are *my* oranges.

Out of Order

1. Late Spring

I see it was not the smug rooms full of lace
or the way verbs settled into the complacency of nouns
or that night I put my head on your lap and we watched
the moon and read its grim diagnosis.

I left you because I got my memory
back. Because I wanted to touch everything,
lie down in dirt, my ribs imprinted in the earth
like fossils. I wanted to become what I loved, fly

into the stunned landscape where clouds unfold
their longings to be lakes and lakes hold clouds in their mouths
as briefly as smoke. But now, below in the derelict city,
artifice is piled upon artifice until what's natural terrifies,
and silverware has the mournful authority of rain.

2. Still Life with Pyramid

One minute we were eating egg rolls
    with hot mustard and listening for thunder
and the next, I felt a snail on my neck,
    but it was the wet place

where your tongue had been.
    Dawn surprises us with its mock fire.
My body like tinder, ready
    to ignite at a touch.

Because it's possible to be alive,
    even in this museum of the dead,

where we marvel that they
    mummified everything—cats, dogs, frogs, mice, beetles.

Because eternity arrives sooner and sooner.
    And miracles struggle against us to appear,
and now it's the end of summer's cash when the trees
    offer their folded green tickets and suddenly

it's no longer terrifying to be separate,
    to see through the transparent wing.

3. *Embellished Table*

A. You read to me from the Psychosomatic Cookbook
B. because we were hungry and had only brought symptoms
    to the table.
C. I could smell twenty-six different odors on your skin and
    clothes.
D. The dry, withholding smell of no sex and barbiturates.
E. The sweet, musky smell of big tips and French wine.
F. The sharp, steely smell of arty talk and large phone bills.
G. The lemon-pepper smell of Sunday with its freshly unwrapped
    saints.
H. Time made us swoon under its insolent weight as we fell
    into each other, full of bones and telepathy,
    and the light squeezed itself into an evening gown
    with the seduction of the half-seen.
I. took note of the details. Even before you left.
J. They gave me the small reprieve of memory.

4. *Declension*

My fever for you was a dwarf star.
I wore a gown made from your sweat.
I used my hands like tourniquets.

You said we could fix it
with crazy glue. The kind the brain
surgeons use on head

wounds when they can't
stop the bleeding. Inside, I led a double life.
Always sleeping, always

awake. My dreams grew legs and walked on land.
From the window days passed,
the color of oysters. Small lakes flashed

in the moonlight like lures. I have always
known the power of what is not
there: that inverted universe where we are loved,

unutterably, by everyone who has failed us.

5. Night Swim, 1974

It's the amnesia of the future,
all the green rooms of summer sealed up.

That's how I saw it then, a failure to be enough,
like a cup of spit you must drink to please your host.

The first time I met him at a party he said, "You know
they're pretty sure the mind

isn't located in the brain," and the night pool we swam in
rippled in the windless air. The ranch house filled with famous poets

and dead poets seemed to be at the party too, with hair
the color of sand, their thought-ghosts flickering in the eucalyptus

leaves. While he explained relativity to me
in layperson's terms, pods split by the pain of carrying their seeds

fell and floated on the water. I pointed out
the *treeness* of the tree, as the frontier

of the party pushed forward onto the patio. The turquoise
pool lights gave him a horror-movie glow, but he

looked so beautiful returning from his own
death, his throat pulsing the way mud does

during rain. I wanted to be his skin's
intricate servant.

The party came to a stalemate,
as they tired of suddenly dull pleasures.

The older male poets had spoken enough
wisdom, the younger gathered around them and

the very drunk had dropped to their knees, possessed
and holy, suffused by that moment

when angels come out of things. And somewhere cherries
ripened in their basket, and the later-to-be-

famous female poet's lemon hair
signaled like a beacon over all of us.

Reasons Not to Have You

—for L.W.

Because I want to go blind in the dark, want the arc
and bite, hungry for what escapes me.

Because I would fold and unfold
in the one light that makes us beads on a string.

Because I am at sea in the earth until I come up breathing,
or in the ocean, so big when I swallow it I get eaten.

Because you are not curious where my words fall
like snow; it is only winter here.

Because I am the nightmare of hair on fire in the mirror,
head full of riddles.

Because my father offered me as a piece of
evidence; I am the corpus delecti.

Because we could just slip our hands between each other's
thighs like passports to another country.

Because you seem to be following me again,
like a verb its noun.

Because I was happy once for a whole
day, overcome by the unpolished copper of your hair.

Because the continent of music is the only one
I want to move to.

Because I want to lie down, a long sleep, then rise
with a gift for my own life.

Borrowed Dress

He left the room, assured of his immortality—
or was it just his cologne?
I once wanted his money—not really his money,
but the freshly minted coins of reason.
His hands smelling like prime numbers.
I once wanted his swagger, his fame
but without the dental work.
I'm reminded that my destiny was
to stand reflected in the infinity-inducing

mirrors with other women in restaurant
bathrooms who pat their hair, make that little
moue with their lips;
who return to the tables of men,
their hands wet, body hairs galvanized
like filaments of iron. Strange how
everything is orderly even in dissipation
when leaves blizzard the pavement.
I don't see them land but their fall,
the *event* of it, is still present, almost invisible.

The Voice

I hear it in the woods, past the stream bed
   filled with rain-loosened stones like obsessive
      thoughts. I know your voice: not the small one in the dirt,
         but the one whipped by salt,
spun-elegant, a slingshot voice that sails over the blue

cataract of dusk. That darkens as water darkens, suddenly
   in changing light with mock threat. I know its doubleness,
      the oak grove's fertile gloom. Its abrupt
         ceremonial kindling. And like fire it tries
to perish without perishing. This is what

I have, not what I wanted: you to solve
   the puzzle of my hair, to wind whatever watch had me ticking
      so close to your ear. But now I think, let us keep
         what distance we have earned. The poem has a difficult,
dark birth, trying to become the body it desires.

The Passion

I would be in love with you right now
if only I hadn't done that already,
the pressure of the horizon

paralyzing. I wanted to take out the shiver-
stick and talk, your head thrown back
like a laughing statue of a god,

your skin lambent, in the damp hotel room
in Germany—there was that moment, under
the pink bedlights, beauty always flying away.

I would take refuge
from the rain in the shadow of the *schloss*,
but I did that already, stood in those big

archaic shadows, so baffling and innocent. I
thought I had a vision at the turn
of the century. For years there was

that moment, the century, its head thrown
back. We were on the unavoidable trail,
the narrow zone we passed through, transfixed

by the blazonry of trees and water. Now
the raft sails through the grotto unharmed, buoyant.
Now we are lost in the old ways of living, splintered

forest, impermeable chambers of the heart: punishment
for forgetfulness. This morning the river was busy
dissembling as I woke suddenly and heard it

as torrents of rain, you, long gone, taking a shower.
Beauty, talk to me, call me by your name.